MW01710744

Triple Threat

Written by Claudette McGowan
Artwork by Tyrus Goshay

Library and Archives Canada Cataloguing in Publication

McGowan, Claudette, author
Triple threat / written by Claudette McGowan ; artwork by Tyrus Goshay.

ISBN 978-0-9812114-8-0 (softcover)

I. Goshay, Tyrus, illustrator II. Title.

PS8625.G68T75 2017 jC813'.6 C2017-900260-0

Cover & Interior Design by Justine Elliott
Artwork by Tyrus Goshay

Excelovate

P.O. Box 34021
RPO Hollandview #7
Aurora, Ontario
L4G 0G3

A girl named Savannah had a dream. It was one she could not forget.

She longed to be a superstar. Also known as a Triple Threat.

A triple threat can act, sing and dance.
In a class above all others.

Savannah wanted to
dazzle the world...
and show off to her
older brothers.

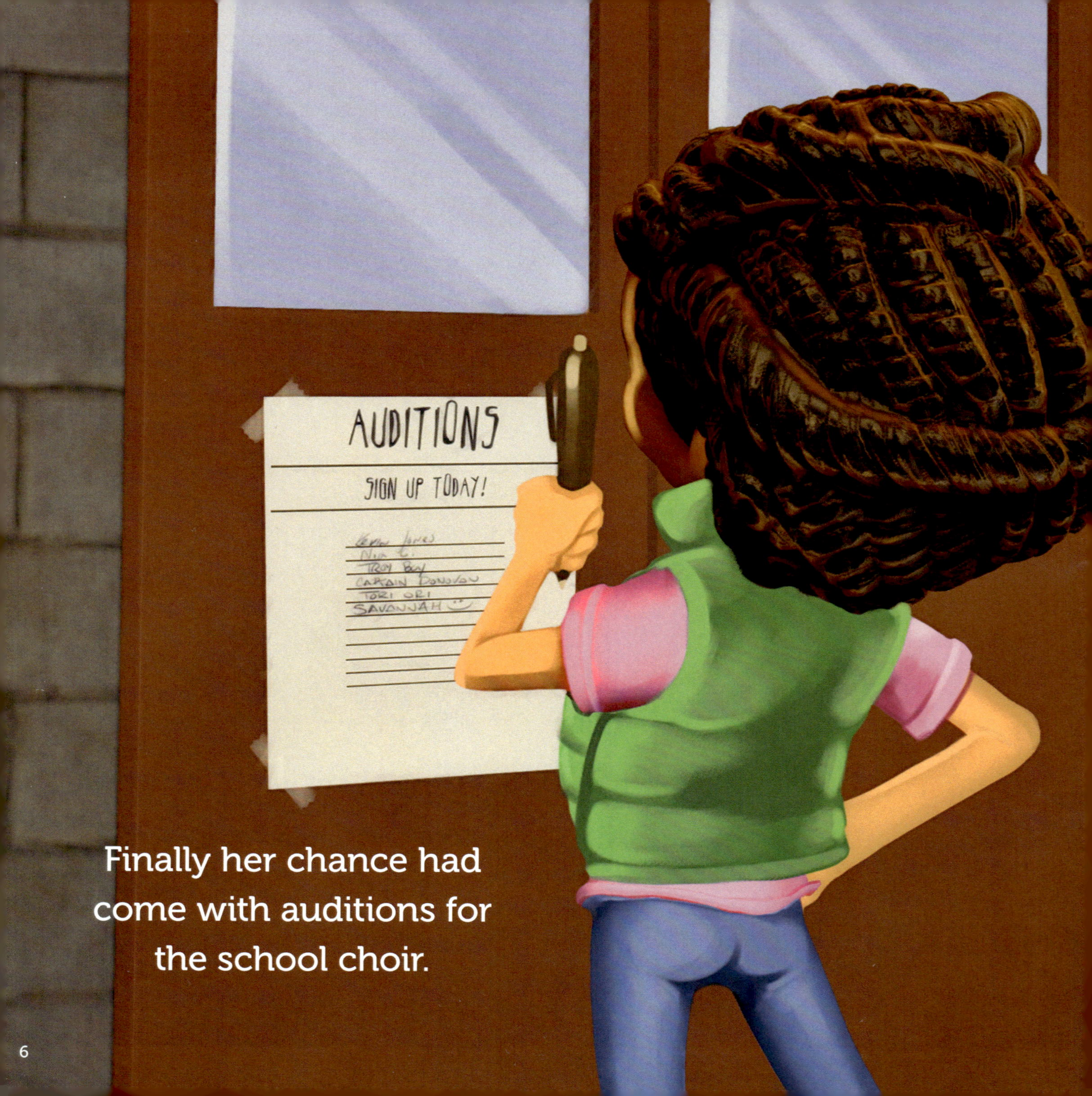

Finally her chance had come with auditions for the school choir.

When she tried to sing, her voice just croaked and her pitch was like a flat tire.

She ran away, her face streaming tears.
This only proved her very worst fears.

“I’m too afraid.
I'm not so good.

I don't measure
up the way
I should!”

As time moved on and
a year went by,
Savannah felt lost and
painfully shy.

Until her cousin reminded her:

"Don't you ever quit. So you had one setback? It's just one setback – that's it!"

The inspiring words were powerful and
gave Savannah the courage to try.

She said, "OK, I'll dance at the next party."
I say why not instead of why.

So the big night arrived.
Savannah was fierce...
twirling and pop-locking.

And all of a sudden - what happened next...

Well, it was absolutely shocking!

Did somebody push her?
Was it a slippery piece of gum?

Everyone witnessed
the horrible moment
when Savannah
slipped and fell flat
on her bum!

Savannah jumped up quickly and darted away. She went into hiding... for at least 1 month, I'd say.

When she returned, she looked
down while walking,
Never smiled or laughed and
avoided all talking.

Her family was saddened. Savannah cut off all her friends.

She thought, Triple Threat... what a joke! More like, Triple Loser is how this ends.

Her older brother decided it
was time to take charge:

"My sister is AMAZING and
her talent is super-large!"

So, he secretly filmed her as
she danced around the yard.

He recorded her singing when she let down her guard.

He knew she
wouldn't be happy.

As usual, she
would call him a
"silly boob."

But he clicked, uploaded and submitted.

Now Savannah is all over YouTube.

5 Views. 100 Views. 1 Million, and growing!!!
America, China, India... where wasn't she showing?

Savannah was discovered and offered her own TV show.

A lead role on Broadway.

Now, she's rolling
in dough!

She is living her dream, and no
one will ever forget...

That Savannah McDougall
is a real Triple Threat.

Savannah